MW00936372

"The Power of Words."
Fight Bullying with Kindness

a book dedicated to teaching young people how to combat bullying, promote inclusiveness and spread the importance of kindness and mutual respect.

Introduction

Dear reader,

You are now facing an extraordinary journey, a journey through the pages of "The Power of Words." This book is more than a collection of words and illustrations; it is an invitation to become agents of change, to build a world where kindness triumphs over cruelty, inclusiveness overcomes indifference, and mutual respect flourishes like a lush garden.

We live in a complex world, and every day we are faced with choices: choosing to be kind, to stand up for those who are most vulnerable, to embrace the differences that make us unique. But we also know that bullying, in its many forms, can cloud the beauty of these choices. That's why we have gathered here, with the goal of giving you the tools to fight bullying, to resist its influence, and to extend a friendly hand to those in need.

"The Power of Words" is a beacon of light in the shadows of bullying, a guide that will take you through stories of challenges and triumphs, of empathy and personal growth. Through these pages, you will discover how every small act of kindness can make a difference, how the power of unity can overcome the brutality of discrimination.

It's not just about talking about bullying; it's about fighting it together. Together we will explore the roots of bullying, analyze its destructive impact, and learn how, through understanding and empathy, we can transform our environment into a safe and welcoming place for all.

We are here to encourage, inspire and guide you along the path to a bullying free future. Every page of this book is an invitation to reflect, grow, and take action. Take part in this adventure, join us, and together we will build a world where respect, kindness and love triumph over all forms of bullying.

We wish you an enlightening read and hope that you, dear reader, can become a proud advocate for a better world.

Chapter 1 "What is Bullying?"

In this chapter, we will explore what it means to be a victim, aggressor, and bystander of bullying. We will use real-life examples and fictional stories to illustrate how bullying can manifest itself in various contexts.

Bullying is an insidious monster that lurks in school hallways, online communities and many other spheres of our daily lives. In this chapter, we will dive into the depths of this complex reality, trying to unveil its many faces and understand the nuances that characterize its presence.

The Victim, the Aggressor and the Spectator

Being a Victim
Imagine you are in a room full of people, but no one seems to notice you. This is the world of those who find themselves bullied. We will explore the emotions, fears and challenges that victims face on

a daily basis, analyzing real stories of boys and girls who have been brave enough to share their experiences.

Being Aggressor

Bullying is not only a problem for those who suffer it, but also for those who perpetrate it. Through real examples, we will try to understand what drives a person to become an aggressor, exploring the psychological and social motives behind such harmful behaviors.

Being a Spectator

Often, bullying unfolds before the eyes of those who prefer to remain silent. We will discover the crucial role of bystanders and how their intervention can make a difference. Stories of bystanders who have found the strength to speak up will show us the potential positive impact of those who choose not to remain passive.

Bullying in Various Contexts

Bullying in School

One of the most common contexts is school, where social dynamics can fuel bullying behavior. We will analyze how bullying manifests itself in the classroom, examining strategies to prevent and address it.

Online Bullying

The digital world offers new opportunities for bullying through cyberbullying and trolling. We will explore how online platforms can become breeding grounds for harmful behavior, encouraging digital awareness and responsibility.

The Power of Stories

Royal Stories

In this chapter, we will address bullying with the powerful weapon of stories. We will hear real voices of those who have experienced bullying firsthand, opening a window into their emotions, dreams, and resilience.

Story 1: Emma, strength in vulnerability

Emma, a young girl of fourteen, decided to share her story of bullying through an online blog. Her decision was an act of courage that inspired many, but behind her brave words were deep emotions and challenges.

Emma had begun bullying in her early teens. The offenses had started with derogatory comments about her body image and had escalated into more insidious forms of cyberbullying. Emma shared the heartbreaking emotions that accompany feeling constantly judged and attacked. Her self-confidence was eroded, and the fear of being constantly under the virtual microscope began to undermine her emotional well-being.

In her testimony, Emma described the sleepless nights, the anxiety that preceded each social media message, and the fear of going to school. But in the midst of this darkness, Emma found strength in vulnerability. With the support of her family and some trusted friends, she decided to share her experience, hoping her story would help other young people feel less alone.

Analysis: Emma faced bullying with courage, turning her vulnerability into strength. Her story highlights the importance of social support in the fight against bullying and shows how exposing problems can be an act of resilience and awareness.

Story 2: Mark, the ally who chose to intervene.
Marco, a 16-year-old youth, witnessed the bullying of a classmate named Alessio. Despite his fear of becoming a target himself, Marco decided to intervene and become an ally for Alessio.

Alessio was being verbally and physically bullied by some classmates. Marco, seized by a sense of empathy and outrage, decided to take action. He began to speak out against bullying, urging his peers to reflect on the consequences of their actions. He also sought the support of teachers and parents, trying to engage the community in the fight against bullying.

Marco's intervention was not without challenges. He faced resistance from some peers and had to deal with the fear of becoming a target for the bullies themselves. However, his determination inspired other kids to join the antibullying cause, turning his act of courage into a resistance movement.

Analysis: Marco's story highlights the vital role of allies in the fight against bullying. His story shows that even a single individual can make a difference, turning fear into action and inspiring others to follow suit. Marco highlighted how empathy and concrete action can be powerful tools in creating safer and more inclusive environments.

Stories of Fiction

Through fictional stories, we will create scenarios that reflect common and real situations. These stories will serve as mirrors through which readers can identify, reflect and develop critical awareness.

Fiction Story 1: Sara, the force behind a screen

Sara, a 15-year-old girl, was a bloom of online creativity. Passionate about drawing and writing, she shared her work on an online platform dedicated to the art community. But behind her bright works lurked a dark side.

One day, Sara started receiving negative and offensive comments on her drawings. Anonymous users were targeting her, criticizing personal aspects of her life and appearance. Initially, Sara tried to ignore these attacks, but as time passed, the venomous words undermined her self-esteem.

Sara decided to confront the situation. With the support of virtual friends and her parents, she shared her experience publicly, writing a post about her struggle with online bullying. She explored the emotions of anger, sadness, and fear she had felt, but also highlighted the strength she had found in facing the situation head-on.

Analysis: Sara's story highlights how online bullying can infiltrate even the most positive places in a person's life. Through her story, we explore the vulnerability of those who share their creativity online and the importance of creating supportive communities that can help counter virtual bullying.

Story of Fiction 2: Luke, the awakening of digital solidarity

Luke, a 16-year-old boy, was an avid online gamer. Through the world of virtual games, he had created friendships with people from all over the world. One day, one of his online friends, Elena, began to be cyberbullied by other gamers.

Luca witnessed the flood of insults and verbal attacks against Elena. Instead of remaining silent, he decided to take a stand. He organized an online solidarity campaign, engaging other players to defend Elena and spread positive messages through the gaming platform.

His initiative caught the attention of the gaming community, sparking a movement against virtual bullying. Even those who initially participated in the offenses joined the cause, making the game a more positive and inclusive environment.

Analysis: Luca's story highlights the potential of digital solidarity in countering online bullying. Through his courage in intervening and mobilizing the virtual community, Luke demonstrated that positive actions can have a significant impact even in the digital world. The story invites us to reflect on the importance of cultivating safer online environments where solidarity can prevail over bullying.

Conclusion of Chapter

Bullying is an enemy that can only be defeated with knowledge and awareness. Through understanding the different perspectives involved, we hope to lay the groundwork for a collective commitment to the fight against bullying. Be prepared for a journey that will take you to explore the dark depths of this phenomenon, but will also ultimately show you the light of hope and change.

Chapter 2 "The Domino Effect."

We will discuss the ripple effect of bullying and how it can affect not only the victim but also the aggressor and bystanders. We will use stories from people who have experienced similar situations and how these experiences have shaped their lives.

Bullying is like a stone thrown into a quiet body of water: its waves spread far beyond the initial point of impact. In this chapter, we will explore the ripple effect of bullying, going beyond the surface to understand how its impact extends, affecting not only the victim, but also the aggressor and bystanders.

The Impact on the Victim

Cycle of Emotion

The victim, in many cases, experiences a whirlwind of emotions, from grief to fear and anger. Through firsthand accounts, we will illustrate how bullying can have a lasting impact on the victim's mental health and emotional well-being.

Testimony 1: Alessia, the burden of invisible scars
Alessia, now 20, experienced bullying during her high school years. The wounds caused by repeated insults to her body image and personality left invisible scars that still affect her mental health today.

Alessia recounts that bullying eroded her self-esteem and fueled a constant sense of negative self-evaluation. Even after leaving school, the emotional scars persist, affecting her ability to form healthy relationships and accept herself.

Fear of judgment and constant anxiety related to social interaction have remained ingrained in Alessia, turning her daily life into an emotional battle. Although she has sought professional help to deal with the trauma of bullying, emotional wounds continue to be a significant part of her story.

Impact on Mental Health: Alessia's testimony reflects the lingering impact of bullying on mental health. The experience during her formative years can leave deep scars that affect self-perception, self-confidence and long-term emotional well-being.

Testimony 2: Marco, the struggle with social anxiety

Marco, 30, experienced bullying during his adolescence, mainly in the form of social exclusion and isolation. Although Marco has built a fulfilling life as an adult, memories of bullying continue to affect his mental health.

Marco developed significant social anxiety because of past experiences. The fear of rejection and the constant need for approval have made it difficult for him to establish meaningful relationships. Although he strives to overcome the effects of bullying, the fear of social interactions continues to impact his daily life.

Impact on Mental Health: Marco's testimony illustrates how bullying can contribute to the development of long-term anxiety disorders. Isolation and lack of social support during critical periods of life can create persistent cycles of anxiety that affect mental health even in adulthood.

In both testimonies, it becomes clear that bullying is not just a problem of the past, but can leave a lasting imprint on the mental health and emotional wellbeing of victims. Awareness of this long-term impact underscores the importance of addressing bullying early and providing the necessary support to victims to help them heal.

Social Cycle

We will explore how bullying can create negative social cycles, affecting an individual's relationships with others. We will tell stories of boys and girls who, because of bullying, have struggled to find a sense of belonging and acceptance.

Story 1: Matthew, the desperate search for acceptance

Matthew, a 15-year-old young man, has experienced years of bullying at school. Because of the constant humiliation and verbal attacks,

Matthew has developed a deep insecurity about his identity and his ability to be accepted by others.

In a desperate attempt to find a sense of belonging, Matthew tried to fit in with popular groups, sacrificing his authenticity. He changed the way he dressed, suppressed his passions and tried to emulate the behavior of bullies to avoid further attacks. However, no matter how hard he tried to conform, Matteo constantly felt excluded and unaccepted.

His struggle to find meaningful connection has had a lasting impact on his selfesteem and his ability to form healthy relationships.

Impact on Relationships: Matthew's story reflects how bullying can push an individual to seek acceptance through conformity, creating a negative cycle in which the desperate search for belonging can lead to further inner conflict and social isolation.

Story 2: Julia, the spiral of isolation.

Giulia, a young 16-year-old girl, was bullied online for her lifestyle choices that did not conform to gender stereotypes. Her passion for music and her unique style of dress made her the target of constant mockery and insults.

Giulia's reaction was to withdraw emotionally and gradually isolate herself from the outside world. Bullying instilled in her the belief that no one understood or accepted her for who she really was. This isolation further fueled her emotional distress, leading to a downward spiral in which fear of judgment reinforced her social detachment.

Impact on Relationships: Julia's story highlights how bullying can contribute to a downward spiral of social isolation. Victims, trying to protect themselves from attacks, may withdraw emotionally, creating barriers that make it difficult to form meaningful bonds with others.

In both stories, bullying profoundly affected Matthew and Julia's ability to make meaningful connections with others. These stories underscore the importance of creating safe and inclusive environments where each individual can feel free to be themselves without fear of judgment or attack.

The Impact on the Aggressor

Psychological Consequences

Bullying can also have serious consequences for those who perpetrate it. We will discuss the psychological challenges that aggressors may face over time, exploring how their behavior affects their perceptions of self and relationships with others.

Story: David, the burden of remorse

David, a teenager, was frequently involved in bullying at school. Initially, his behavior seemed to be fueled by a search for approval from his peers and a desire to be seen as "strong" by his friends.

However, over time, his involvement in bullying began to take a toll on his mental health.

David began to feel guilt and remorse for the pain he was inflicting on others. Although he tried to hide these feelings behind a facade of indifference, his awareness of the harm he was causing began to undermine his self-esteem. His relationships with friends became strained, as many distanced him because of his aggressive behavior.

Over time, David began to struggle with social isolation and a lack of meaningful connections. He began to perceive himself as a bad person, unable to change and deserving of being ostracized. His journey highlighted the psychological challenges that abusers can face over time, including the weight of remorse and distorted self-perception.

Impact on Attacker's Mental Health: David's story illustrates how aggressors can face serious psychological challenges over time. Guilt, loss of social connections, and negative self-perception can become part of their experience, suggesting that bullying can also have lasting consequences for those who perpetrate it.

These stories underscore the importance of early intervention, not only to support victims of bullying but also to provide perpetrators with the resources they need to reflect, learn and change their behavior in order to avoid serious long-term consequences.

Empathy Cycle

Through stories of those who were aggressors and then chose the path of empathy, we will show that there is a possibility to break the cycle of bullying and turn negativity into a path of personal growth.

Story: Frederick, from negativity to empathy

Federico, a young man who had once actively participated in bullying during his adolescence, embarked on a remarkable journey of personal growth. Initially involved in bullying to try to fit in with a group, Federico began to reflect on the consequences of his behaviors after being subjected to similar actions in a different context.

The turning point came when Federico began participating in educational programs on mindfulness and empathy. Through learning experiences that highlighted the impact of bullying on the mental health and emotional wellbeing of victims, Federico began to see his past actions with different eyes.

As he increasingly understood the pain inflicted on victims, Frederick decided to take an active stance to break the cycle of bullying. He began participating in bullying prevention projects in schools, sharing his experience to show others that change is possible and that past actions do not have to define the future.

Frederick also tried to make amends for his mistakes by apologizing to the people he had hurt in the past. This act of responsibility and his commitment to empathy enabled him to build new relationships based on sincerity and mutual understanding.

Turning Negativity into Personal Growth: Federico's story is a powerful example of breaking the cycle of bullying and turning negativity into personal growth. Awareness of his own past actions, combined with the empathy he gained, provided Federico with the tools to embark on a path of positive change.

This story highlights that, even for those who have been aggressors, there is an opportunity to redeem themselves, learn from the experience, and become agents of positive change. Empathy and taking responsibility can be powerful catalysts for transforming negativity into a path of personal growth, demonstrating that true strength lies in the ability to change and the desire to contribute to a better world.

The Impact on Spectators

The Weight of Passivity

Viewers, in turn, may feel trapped in a moral dilemma. We will examine how passivity can contribute to the expansion of the domino effect and how, through small acts of courage, viewers can change the course of events.

Story: Martina, from bystander to change agent
Martina, a 16-year-old girl, had always silently witnessed bullying at her school. She feared becoming a target if she raised her voice or defended the victims. Fear of judgment from others and a desire to avoid conflict had kept her passive in the face of harmful behavior.

Everything changed when one of her closest friends, Giulia, became the main victim of a group of bullies. Martina, despite her fear, felt it was time to take action. She started with small gestures of support, such as sharing positive messages about Giulia on social media and offering her company during difficult times.

Martina also involved other friends, trying to create a united front against bullying. They organized a student assembly to raise awareness of the issue and encourage the community to speak out against bullying. Despite her initial fear, Martina found that many students shared her desire for change.

Thanks to the courage of Martina and others who joined her, the school culture began to change. Resistance against bullying has grown, and awareness of collective responsibility in bullying prevention has led to greater cohesion in the school community.

The Power of Small Gestures of Courage: Martina's story demonstrates how even a seemingly powerless bystander can become an agent of change through small gestures of courage. Passivity can contribute to the expanding domino effect of bullying, but decisive and responsible action by bystanders can break this negative cycle.

Viewers, even with seemingly insignificant gestures, can change the course of events. Moral support, sharing positive messages, and creating a culture of resistance can turn viewers into active allies, demonstrating that positive change can begin with small steps of courage.

The Active Role of Spectators

Stories of bystanders who decided to take action, becoming agents of change, will illustrate how empathy and solidarity can break the negative cycle of bullying.

Story 1: Alexander, the empathy that changed destiny

Alexander, a 14-year-old student, was a silent bystander to bullying involving his classmate, Sofia. One day, he witnessed a particularly brutal incident in which Sofia was targeted by a group of bullies. Despite his fear of becoming the next target, Alexander felt the urge to do something about it.

Instead of remaining silent, Alexander decided to approach Sofia after the episode. He showed empathy and offered her support. Together, they shared the experience with a trusted teacher, who initiated an intervention against bullying. Alexander's action inspired other classmates to break their silence, turning solidarity into a unified front against bullying.

His empathy helped change Sofia's fate and created a chain of events that led to greater awareness and prevention of bullying in the school.

Story 2: Clare, the solidarity that built bridges

Chiara, a 17-year-old youth, became a witness to the humiliation suffered by Luca, a classmate, because of his sexual orientation. Initially, Chiara was afraid to intervene, fearing judgment from other students. However, her compassion overcame her fear.

Chiara decided to approach Luca and offer him support. She also involved a group of trusted friends to create a supportive environment around Luca. Together, they worked to raise the school's awareness of the importance of inclusivity and diversity.

Clare's solidarity has had a profound impact on Luke's life. Not only did it help stop the bullying of him, but it also created a more welcoming environment for all students, promoting understanding and tolerance.

Empathy and Solidarity as Agents of Change: Both stories illustrate how bystanders' empathy and solidarity can break the negative cycle of bullying. Choosing to intervene, even with small gestures of support, has the power to change the course of events and transform the culture of the community.

These stories demonstrate that compassion can build bridges, inspire courageous action, and create an environment where bullying does not find fertile ground. Viewer empathy can become a catalyst for change, demonstrating that everyone has a role to play in fostering a culture of respect, inclusion, and solidarity.

Stories of Transformation

Resilience and Revival

We will conclude the chapter with stories of individuals who, despite experiencing bullying, have managed to transform their experience into a path of growth and resilience. These stories will serve as inspiration for anyone facing bullying.

Story 1: Marta, strength in diversity

Marta, a 16-year-old youth, experienced bullying because of her cultural diversity. Having grown up in a multicultural environment, Marta brought with her different traditions and customs. However, this diversity made her the target of derision and negative comments from her peers.

Instead of bowing to pressure, Marta decided to embrace her cultural identity and turn her experience of bullying into a path of growth. She began to openly share her experiences with other students, educating them about the richness of diversity and challenging stereotypes.

Marta also involved teachers and parents in promoting a more inclusive school environment. Her leadership has inspired a cultural change in the school, promoting tolerance and acceptance of differences. Marta has turned her experience of bullying into a mission to build bridges between people and celebrate diversity.

Story 2: John, resilience through passion

John, a 15-year-old boy, faced bullying because of his passion for theater and acting. His creative spirit and dedication to the stage were the object of ridicule by some classmates who did not understand his passion.

Instead of abandoning his art, John decided to channel negativity into strength. He continued to pursue his passion, participating in local theater productions and building a network of friends who shared his interests. His dedication to theater provided him with a safe and supportive space, allowing him to develop resilience and self-esteem.

John also began to share his story, using his bullying experience as inspiration for other young artists. His story has become an example of how resilience through passion can transform the experience of bullying into a source of personal strength and growth.

Inspiration through Resilience: Both stories demonstrate that despite bullying, it is possible to transform the experience into a path of growth and resilience. Marta and John demonstrated that embracing one's identity, persevering in passions, and sharing one's experiences can be powerful ways to overcome bullying and inspire others to do the same.

These stories serve as positive examples for anyone facing bullying, showing that it is possible to emerge from these difficulties stronger, aware and ready to contribute to a more inclusive and respectful environment.

Conclusion of Chapter

The domino effect of bullying is a complex but not insuperable reality. Through understanding the many facets of this phenomenon, we hope to motivate readers to become aware of their roles in the fight against bullying. Positive change can begin with small but meaningful gestures, and together we can reverse the tide of the domino effect by promoting a culture of respect and kindness.

Chapter 3 "Diversity and Inclusion."

We will explore the concept of diversity and how we can embrace and celebrate the differences among us. Stories will be included of characters who have learned to appreciate diversity and be open to the experiences of others.

Diversity is the richness of our humanity, and inclusion is the bridge that unites us, allowing us to walk together. In this chapter, we will explore the deeper meaning of diversity and inclusion, learning to celebrate the differences that make each individual unique.

Understanding Diversity

The Human Mosaic

Imagine the world as a large mosaic, composed of unique and colorful pieces. We will explore the concept of diversity as an opportunity, not only to tolerate, but to appreciate and embrace cultural, ethnic, gender and other differences.

Imagine the world as an immense mosaic, a vibrant composition of unique and colorful pieces, each carrying a unique history, tradition, and diversity. Each tile, regardless of its shape or color, contributes to a richer, more complex picture. This mosaic is our humanity, an intricate weaving of cultural, ethnic, gender and many other nuances that reflect the extraordinary diversity present in the world.

Diversity should not be seen as a barrier or obstacle, but rather as an opportunity. Each element of the mosaic has the power to enrich our understanding of the world, open us to new perspectives and nurture our capacity for empathy. Embracing diversity means not just tolerating differences, but celebrating them, recognizing the intrinsic value of each individual and their unique experiences.

In this mosaic, diverse cultural nuances offer us a rich and varied overview of the traditions that enrich our global heritage. Ethnic diversity teaches us that beauty lies in the multiplicity of origins and histories that form the fabric of our society. Gender differences show us that strength and wisdom can flourish regardless of category.

When we recognize and embrace diversity, we open ourselves to a world of possibilities. We learn to see beyond external appearances, to overcome prejudices and stereotypes, and to understand that the true richness of our existence lies in the vastness of human experience. Diversity offers us the opportunity to learn, grow and thrive together, turning the mosaic of the world into a collective masterpiece.

In this scenario, tolerance becomes an important first step, but the ultimate goal is the opening of the heart and mind to sincere appreciation of differences. Embracing diversity is an act of wisdom that inspires us to build authentic connections, create inclusive environments, and work together for a future where everyone can contribute their own unique color to the global mosaic, making the world a more vibrant and harmonious place.

Fight Against Stereotypes

We will address stereotypes that can fuel bullying. We will use stories of characters who have challenged cultural and gender stereotypes, demonstrating that each individual is unique beyond superficial labels.

Story 1: Aisha, strength beyond cultural stereotypes

Aisha, a young woman from a family with diverse cultural roots, has faced cultural stereotypes since childhood. While growing up, Aisha was often subjected to prejudices and stereotypes related to her ethnic background. Many assumed that she had certain cultural expectations or followed particular traditions, without taking into consideration her individuality.

Determined to challenge these stereotypes, Aisha embarked on a journey of self-exploration and defining her identity. She chose to pursue her personal passions and interests, pushing the boundaries of the cultural stereotypes that surrounded her. Aisha demonstrated that an individual's strength cannot be encased in predefined cultural categories or expectations, but goes beyond them, rooting herself in her authenticity and uniqueness.

Through her efforts to combat cultural stereotypes, Aisha has inspired others to see beyond superficial labels and recognize the importance of embracing the richness of individual diversity.

Story 2: Luke, breaking gender stereotypes through art

Luca, a young man with a passion for dance, faced gender stereotypes that limited his freedom of expression. In a society that often associates dance with rigidly defined gender stereotypes, Luca challenged the prejudice that saw dance as an art form reserved only for women or a certain type of masculinity.

Despite the criticism and judgment, Luke has continued to follow his passion for dance. Through his performances, he has demonstrated that art has no gender and that dance can be a form of expression accessible to anyone, regardless of gender. His dedication has opened new perspectives on masculinity, breaking cultural stereotypes that limit individuals' range of expression.

Aisha and Luca's stories teach us that the strength and beauty of each individual goes beyond cultural and gender stereotypes. Each person is unique, with the ability to define his or her own identity beyond superficial social expectations. Challenging stereotypes not only frees individuals from the restriction of labels, but also enriches society, allowing everyone to express themselves fully and be appreciated for who they truly are.

Celebrating Differences

A Concert of Voices

We will explore stories of people from diverse backgrounds, telling how they have learned to celebrate their diversity. Examples will be included of communities that have embraced diversity as a positive force, creating an environment where every voice is valued.

Story 1: Samir and Valeria, a bond beyond cultural differences

Samir, originally from a Middle Eastern country, and Valeria, who was born and raised in a small European village, went through completely different life stories. When they first met during a cultural exchange program, they faced stereotypes and prejudices related to their different origins.

Instead of allowing these differences to create barriers, Samir and Valeria chose to celebrate their diversity. They began to share their traditions, discovering the similarities that linked their cultures instead of focusing on the differences. They organized cultural events in their community, engaging people and inviting them to explore and appreciate the uniqueness of their respective heritages.

Their initiative has inspired the community to embrace diversity as a source of enrichment. Multicultural events have become a point of pride for the community, creating an environment where every voice is heard and every tradition is valued. Celebrating diversity has become a key element in building a more inclusive and respectful community.

Story 2: Aisha and Carlos, a connection that crosses language barriers

Aisha, born in an Asian country, and Carlos, a Latino boy, met in an urban, multicultural setting. Although they came from different linguistic backgrounds, together they faced the challenge of overcoming language barriers to celebrate their diversity.

Aisha and Carlos created a language exchange group in their community, inviting people from different backgrounds to share their languages and cultures. This led to a series of events where people learned from each other and discovered the importance of celebrating linguistic and cultural diversity.

Their initiative permeated the community, resulting in an environment where every language and culture was considered a valuable resource. People learned to value diversity as an opportunity for continued growth and learning. This celebration of diversity created a stronger and resiliently connected social fabric.

These stories demonstrate that when people learn to celebrate diversity, they can transform their communities into places of continuous learning, mutual respect, and authentic connection. In an environment where every voice is valued, diversity becomes a positive force that enriches everyone's lives and helps build a more inclusive and welcoming society.

Embracing Inclusion

We will illustrate the importance of creating inclusive environments, where every individual feels accepted and empathetically understood. We will tell stories of communities and institutions that have adopted inclusive policies and practices, demonstrating that inclusion is an investment in the common good.

Story 1: St. George's Inclusive School.

St. George School, in a small community, decided to embrace an inclusive approach to accommodate students of all abilities and backgrounds. This decision stemmed from the realization that each individual has unique value and that education should be a right accessible to all.

The school has implemented personalized learning programs that are tailored to the individual needs of students. In addition, safe spaces were created to promote awareness and acceptance of diversity. Teachers received training on inclusion and the differentiated approach, ensuring that every student felt supported and valued.

The result has been a vibrant school environment where students learn not only from textbooks but also from the experiences and perspectives of their classmates. The surrounding community has responded positively, recognizing that investing in inclusive education is a step toward creating knowledgeable and supportive citizens.

Story 2: Rivertown's Inclusive Company.

A Rivertown manufacturing company has embraced inclusion as an integral part of its business philosophy. Leadership has recognized the value of employee diversity and created a work environment that reflects this vision.

The company implemented inclusive hiring policies, ensuring equal opportunities for people of different ages, cultural backgrounds, abilities, and sexual orientations. Inclusion training initiatives were introduced to ensure that every employee felt respected and understood. In addition, lines of communication were opened to accommodate the perspectives and needs of all team members.

The effect of these policies has been evident in increased employee satisfaction, reduced absenteeism, and increased creativity and efficiency. The community has recognized the company as a model of best practices, demonstrating that inclusion is not only an investment in employee well-being, but also a competitive advantage and a positive contribution to the community.

Both of these stories illustrate how inclusion not only enriches the lives of specific individuals but also contributes to the common good, creating stronger communities, more resilient institutions, and a world in which every individual is recognized, accepted, and empathetically understood.

Opening the Mind to Empathy

Looking Through the Eyes of Others

We will explore the concept of empathy as a key to understanding the experiences of others. Stories of characters who have learned to open their minds to empathy will show us how this can be a powerful antidote to bullying.

Building Bridges, Not Walls

We will discuss how building bridges between people instead of erecting walls can promote a culture of mutual respect. Stories of unlikely friendships and unexpected connections will show that inclusion can be the key to a more united world.

Story 1: The Bridge Between Generations

In a small neighborhood, there was an elderly gentleman named John and a young teenager named Matthew. Initially, it seemed that their lives did not have much in common. John was an old man with a rich life story, while Matthew was a teenager who was passionate about technology and contemporary music.

One day, during a community project to improve the local park, John and Matthew found themselves working together. Initially, there were barriers of understanding and differences in interest, but they soon discovered that each had something unique to offer.

John shared his life experiences, teaching Matteo lessons learned through the years. In return, Matthew introduced John to the latest technologies and modern music. Their friendship has grown, becoming an example of how building bridges between generations can lead to deeper understanding and authentic connection.

This unexpected friendship has inspired other community members to seek connections with people of different ages. The neighborhood has become a place where generational barriers have been broken down, creating an environment where each individual's life stories are appreciated and respected.

Story 2: Union across Cultural Differences.

In a big city, there were two families who came from completely different cultural backgrounds. Sofia's family, an immigrant from Asia, moved next door to Marco's family, originally from Latin

America. Initially, there were language and cultural barriers that made communication difficult.

However, rather than closing in on themselves, the two families chose to break down the walls of difference. They held shared dinners where they shared their traditional foods, learned each other's languages and celebrated cultural holidays with each other.

Through this cultural exchange, the families discovered that, despite appearances, they shared many core values and common goals for their children's future. This unexpected connection led to deep friendships and demonstrated that inclusion can be the key to building a more united world, where cultural differences become a source of richness and mutual learning.

Both stories illustrate how building bridges between seemingly different people can lead to meaningful connections and foster a culture of mutual respect. In a world united by human connections, inclusion becomes a driving force that breaks down walls of ignorance and intolerance, building bridges of understanding and friendship.

Conclusion of Chapter

The chapter on diversity and inclusion teaches us that the beauty of our world lies in its variety. Working together to embrace differences not only enriches our lives, but creates an atmosphere of mutual respect and understanding. In this chapter, we have seen how stories of open-mindedness and acceptance can be a guide for all of us. We hope readers can take these lessons into their own lives, promoting a world where everyone is free to be themselves without fear of judgment.

Chapter 4 "Be an Ally"

In this chapter, we will provide practical advice on how to be an ally for those who are bullied. We will tell stories of friendships that have developed through solidarity and mutual help.

Being an ally is an act of courage and compassion. In this chapter, we will explore the deeper meaning of being an ally for those who are bullied, providing practical advice and inspiring readers to become agents of change in the lives of others.

Understanding the Role of the Ally

The Strength of the Ally

We will introduce the concept of allies as anyone who chooses to be on the side of those being bullied. We will explore the power of friendship and solidarity as key tools in the fight against bullying.

Welcome to chapter 4 of Together Against Bullying. In this chapter, we will explore the deeper meaning of being an ally in the fight against bullying. Being an ally means choosing to stand with those who are bullied, to raise your voice against injustice, and to build an environment where solidarity and friendship are the main weapons against bullying.

The Importance of Allies

Being an ally is more than a gesture, it is an active commitment to creating a world in which every individual feels supported and respected. Allies are the foundation upon which an inclusive and respectful community is built, ready to counter bullying in all its forms.

The Power of Friendship

Friendship is one of the most powerful tools in the fight against bullying. When we come together as friends, we create a united front that makes it difficult for bullying to take root. Over the next few pages, we will explore stories of friendships that have become bastions of resistance against bullying, demonstrating that friendship can turn into a powerful ally in the fight against injustice.

Stories of Solidarity

The Ally Team: At one school, a group of students came together to form the "Ally Team." They pledged to intervene whenever they saw bullying situations, offering support to those in need. This team not only made the school a safer place, but also proved that even small acts of solidarity can have a lasting impact.

The Listening Friend: In another story, a boy named Luca discovered that his friend Martina was being bullied online. Instead of remaining silent, Luca became an attentive listener, offering his support and encouraging Martina to talk to trusted adults. This story teaches us that being an ally can also mean being a friend who listens and supports.

Be an Ally, Be a Friend

Finally, remember that being an ally does not require grand gestures, but rather a willingness to be there for others. In this chapter, we will explore how each of us can become a powerful ally, helping to create an environment where solidarity and friendship are the keys to defeating bullying.

The Allied Responsibility

We will discuss the responsibility associated with being an ally, emphasizing the importance of acting proactively and being a positive voice in countering bullying.

Practical Tips for Being an Ally

Active Listening

Listening is an act of kindness. We will provide suggestions on how to practice active listening, a critical skill for understanding the experiences of those being bullied.

Intervene with Wisdom

We will outline effective ways to intervene when witnessing bullying, encouraging allies to be present and offer support in a positive way. Spreading Kindness

Kindness is contagious. We will offer practical ideas on how to spread kindness around, creating an environment that counteracts bullying.

Stories of Friendships that Change the Game

Friendships that Defy Bullying

We will tell stories of friendships that have defied bullying, demonstrating how mutual support can be a transformative force.

The Power of Unity

We will explore how solidarity among friends and allies can form a unified front against bullying, demonstrating that unity is an insuperable force.

Conclusion of Chapter

The chapter "Be an Ally" ends with an invitation: a call for every reader to become an active ally in the fight against bullying. Being an ally is not just a role, but a daily commitment to creating an environment where kindness prevails over cruelty. Through the power of stories of game-changing friendships, we hope readers can find inspiration to be the allies the world so desperately needs.

Chapter 5 "Combating Bullying: Tangible Actions."

Welcome to chapter 5 of Together Against Bullying. In this chapter, we will explore tangible actions that each of us can take to combat bullying individually and collectively. Through practical tips and strategies based on the experience of those who have faced bullying, we will learn how to turn willingness to act into concrete actions.

Tips for Combating Bullying on an Individual Level

Talk and Share: Don't remain silent in the face of bullying. Talk to someone you trust-a friend, teacher, or parent. Sharing your experience is the first step to getting support.

Create Awareness: Use social media or organize events in your school or community to raise awareness about bullying. Awareness is key to creating an environment that rejects intimidating behavior.

Practice Empathy: Seek to understand the feelings of others. Empathy can create deeper connections and help break the cycle of bullying.

Set Limits: If you witness bullying, clearly state that such behavior is not acceptable. Your voice can make a difference in creating an environment where mutual respect is the norm.

The Importance of Self-Esteem and Authenticity.

Self-esteem is the foundation on which we build our identity and face life's challenges. It is crucial in protecting against the negative impact of bullying. Authenticity, on the other hand, allows us to be true to ourselves and others, creating an environment in which diversity is celebrated and bullying cannot thrive.

Tips for Developing a Strong Personal Identity:

Accept Yourself: Recognize and embrace your uniqueness. Accepting yourself is the first step in building solid self-esteem.

Define Your Values: Reflect on the values that are important to you. Living consistently with your values will help build a solid foundation for your identity.

Create Realistic Goals: Set realistic and attainable goals. Success in small daily challenges will help boost your self-esteem over time.

Cultivate Positive Relationships: Surround yourself with people who support and encourage you. Positive relationships can play a key role in building self-esteem.

Tips for Inspiring Authenticity.

Promote Acceptance: Promote an environment where diversity is accepted and celebrated. This creates a space where everyone feels free to be authentic.

Encourage Individual Talents: Recognize and encourage individual talents. This helps people feel valued for who they are, helping to strengthen their selfesteem.

Be a Model of Authenticity: Show authenticity in your daily life. Being a positive role model can inspire others to do the same.

In conclusion, building self-esteem and authenticity not only protects against the impact of bullying, but also helps create an environment where diversity is valued. Together, we can cultivate a culture of respect and acceptance, making it harder for bullying to take root in our communities.

Testimonies of Resilience

Sofia's story: Sofia faced bullying at school because of her passion for science. With the support of teachers and the involvement of other students, she created a science club that promoted diversity and helped change the school culture.

Matthew's experience: Matthew, after dealing with bullying, started an outreach project in his community. He organized meetings and events to engage others and proved that the actions of a single person can have a significant impact.

Sara's Strength: Sara faced bullying because of her talent for dance. By accepting herself and maintaining her passion, she built self-esteem that protected her from the negative impact of bullying. Her authenticity inspired others to do the same.

Marco's Identity: Marco has learned to define his identity beyond the expectations of others. He developed strong self-esteem based on his authenticity, becoming an example of how self-confidence can fend off bullying.

The Emotional Impact of Bullying.

Bullying can generate a range of negative emotions, such as anger, sadness, and anxiety. Managing these emotions is crucial for emotional well-being and resilience.

Tips for Dealing with Emotions

Reading As Emotional Vent: Reading can be a powerful way to express and deal with emotions. Finding books that address similar issues can help you feel understood and gain different perspectives.

Art As a Form of Expression: Art creation, such as drawing, painting or writing, can be a therapeutic means of expressing difficult emotions. This allows pain to be transformed into something creative and constructive.

Physical Activities As an outlet: Exercise is an effective way to release stress and negative emotions. Walking, running or playing a sport can help channel energy in a positive way.

Create a Support Network: Talk to friends, family members or trusted counselors. Having a support network can help you share emotions, receive comfort and get helpful advice.

Stories of Emotional Liberation

Giulia's Journey: Giulia, after experiencing episodes of bullying, began to write a journal in which she expressed her emotions. This act of writing allowed her to better understand her feelings and contributed to her emotional healing.

Luca's Art: Luca, who is passionate about drawing, has turned his negative experiences into works of art. This form of artistic expression not only allowed him to process emotions, but also inspired others to do the same.

Tips for Emotional Expression

Find Your Form of Expression: Experiment with different creative activities and find the one that resonates best with you. Everyone has a unique way of expressing emotions.

Art and Reading Programs: Participate in programs that encourage art and reading as tools for expression. Many communities offer workshops and initiatives to support emotional management.

Create a Safe Space: Create a safe space where you can freely express your emotions without judgment. This can be physical, such as a quiet room, or virtual, such as a supportive online community.

In conclusion, managing emotions is key to dealing with the emotional impact of bullying. Using creative tools such as reading and art, we can turn pain into strength, promoting emotional healing and resilience. Together, we can build an environment that values emotional expression as an integral part of our mental health.

Collective Strategies Against Bullying

Awareness Programs: Work with teachers and administrators to implement bullying awareness programs in your school. These programs can educate students about the consequences of bullying and promote a culture of respect.

Training for Teachers and Staff: Ensure that teachers and school staff are properly trained to deal with bullying. Training can include intervention strategies and techniques for dealing with difficult situations.

Support Groups: Create or participate in anti-bullying support groups. These groups provide a safe space for those who have been bullied or who wish to be active in the fight against it.

Practical Conclusions

The fight against bullying requires concrete and courageous actions. In this chapter, we will explore practical tips and strategies that will enable readers to become active agents in creating a bullying-free environment. Testimonials from those who have faced bullying will offer inspiration and guidance for anyone facing similar situations.

Conclusion of Chapter

The chapter "Combating Bullying: Tangible Actions" concludes with an invitation to translate words into action. Each reader is encouraged to take the helm of his or her own life and the environment around them. Through tangible actions, awareness and a culture of collective resistance, we hope this chapter will inspire positive changes that will spread like a wave against bullying. May each reader find strength in the testimonies of those who have faced bullying, and may these stories be catalysts for personal and social transformation.

Chapter 6 "Empathy As a Key to Connection."

Empathy is more than just an intellectual understanding of the emotions of others; it is the ability to connect deeply with the experiences of others. This quality plays a crucial role in countering bullying because it creates human bonds that go beyond superficial barriers.

Stories of Transformative Empathy

Elena's Transformation: Elena, a shy student, witnessed the bullying of a classmate. Instead of remaining silent, she decided to approach him, offering friendship and support. Her empathy not only changed the victim's life, but also positively affected the viewers, creating an atmosphere of solidarity.

Paul's Initiative: Paul, after witnessing an act of bullying, initiated a project at his school to promote mutual understanding. Through activities that encouraged empathy, he helped create an environment where differences were celebrated rather than denigrated.

Role of Empathy in Promoting Respect

Understanding Diverse Perspectives: Empathy invites us to understand the different perspectives of others, breaking down the barriers of lack of understanding and prejudice.

Fostering Solidarity: Stories of empathy inspire solidarity. When we put ourselves in the shoes of others, we are more likely to stand up for those who are bullied and foster a culture of mutual respect.

Building Meaningful Relationships: Empathy is the foundation of meaningful relationships. Cultivating this quality not only protects against isolation but also helps create human bonds that withstand challenges.

Strategies for Cultivating Empathy

Practicing Active Listening: Listening carefully is the first step to understanding the experiences of others.

Reading Stories of Diversity: Reading stories that reflect diverse experiences helps develop broader empathy.

Participate in Intercultural Experiences: Getting involved in experiences that expose you to different cultures helps you understand the challenges and joys of others.

Promoting Open Conversation: Creating spaces where people can openly discuss their experiences promotes an environment of mutual trust and understanding.

In conclusion, empathy is a powerful force that can transform the way we relate to others and counteract bullying. Through stories of transformative empathy, we hope to inspire readers to cultivate this quality, creating a world in which mutual understanding and respect are the pillars of our culture.

Chapter 7 "Looking to the Future"

Welcome to the final chapter of Together Against Bullying. In this chapter, we turn to the future with hope and determination. We will explore the possibilities of a world without bullying, emphasizing how each of us can help create an environment that celebrates individuality and promotes inclusiveness.

Reflection on Progress

Looking to the future allows us to reflect on the progress we have made in the fight against bullying. Communities and individuals around the world are demonstrating that change is possible, and our collective efforts can transform reality.

Examples of Resilient Communities

Rivertown Community: Rivertown has addressed bullying through inclusive education programs in schools and activities that promote mutual understanding. This community has demonstrated that an integrated approach can create a safe and welcoming school environment.

Crescent City Initiative: Crescent City has adopted a zero-tolerance policy for bullying, actively involving parents, teachers and students in anti-bullying programs. This approach has led to a significant decrease in bullying incidents in the community.

The Power of Individual Change

Each of us can contribute to a future without bullying through daily actions. Here's how:

Promoting Inclusiveness

Be open and welcoming to all, celebrating differences and accepting diversity as a value.

Being an Ally

Be an ally for those being bullied, intervening in a positive way and offering support.

Spreading Awareness

Continue to raise awareness of the seriousness of bullying through participation in community initiatives and sharing success stories.

Educating New Generations

Engage youth in educational programs that teach respect, tolerance and the importance of kindness.

Hope and Action

We end this journey with the knowledge that the future is in our hands. Each of us can be an integral part of change, helping to build a world where bullying is just a thing of the past. We are bearers of hope, agents of change and creators of a bullying-free future.

The Power of Collectivity

As we look to the future, let us remember that the strength of community overcomes any form of bullying. Together, we can shape an environment that embraces diversity, promotes inclusiveness and inspires future generations to do the same.

Our commitment today is the foundation of a bullying-free tomorrow. With this positive vision, we close this book with the hope that everyone can be part of this transformation, paving the way for a future where respect and love prevail over all forms of bullying.

Conclusion of the Book

Dear Readers,

This journey through the pages of "The Power of Words" now comes to its end, but our call to hope and action continues to echo in your minds. We have reached the point where the past and the present meet, opening the door to a future where bullying will be just a thing of the past, a page turned in human history.

We look forward with confidence, aware of the power each reader possesses to shape the course of events. We have explored the roots of bullying, analyzed its devastating impact and presented concrete strategies to counter it. But now, more than ever, it is time to take action.

The testimonies of communities that have successfully dealt with bullying light the way for us. They have shown that kindness, solidarity and inclusion can be the winning tools in building a bullying-free environment. Positive initiatives are already shaping our world, demonstrating that change is possible when we engage collectively.

The future is in your hands, in the hands of those who embrace the healthy principle of inclusion and spread the light of kindness. Every action, no matter how small, contributes to positive change. Every kind word, every gesture of solidarity, every act of courage in confronting bullying is a brick in the building of a better world.

We close this journey with the hope that each of you will feel called to be part of this transformation. Be the architects of change, the advocates of empathy, and the allies of victims of bullying. Each step we take together brings us closer to a future where kindness, respect and inclusion are the pillars of our society.

We thank you for sharing this journey with us. Go forward with the knowledge that your commitment makes a difference. Be bearers of hope, agents of change and ambassadors of kindness.

The future is bright when we engage Together Against Bullying.

INDEX

Any other references in this text, to names of persons, quotations, places, events, titles, historical facts, whether they really existed or existed are to be considered purely coincidental and for narrative purposes only, taken possibly in part from public sources and/or on free-viewing information sites.

Reproduction and translation rights are reserved. No part of this book may be used, reproduced or disseminated by any means without written permission from the Author and/or Ediluma Ltd. Reproduction, even in part, is prohibited.

Title: The Power of Words - Author: mdv - Edition 2023
Publisher Ediluma Ltd
Suite 24Tax 137B; West Link House 981 Great West Road; TW89DN Brentford -
Electronic Mail: ediluma@yahoo.com

Ediluma
Professional publishing

Made in the USA
Las Vegas, NV
13 February 2024

85736787R00046